AN ECCENTRIC ECLECTIC COLLECTION

A BOOK OF POEMS

JEREMIAH 'BULLFROG' WILMOT

An Eccentric Eclectic Collection
Copyright © 2024 by Jeremiah 'Bullfrog' Wilmot.

All rights reserved. No part of this publication may be reproduced, distributed, or transmitted in any form or by any means, including photocopying, recording, or other electronic or mechanical methods, without the written consent of the publisher. The only exceptions are for brief quotations included in critical reviews and other noncommercial uses permitted by copyright law.

MILTON & HUGO L.L.C.
4407 Park Ave., Suite 5
Union City, NJ 07087, USA

Website: *www. miltonandhugo.com*
Hotline: *1- 888-778-0033*
Email: *info@miltonandhugo.com*

Ordering Information:
Quantity sales. Special discounts are granted to corporations, associations, and other organizations. For more information on these discounts, please reach out to the publisher using the contact information provided above.

Library of Congress Control Number:		2024911486
ISBN-13:	979-8-89285-184-8	[Paperback Edition]
	979-8-89285-185-5	[Digital Edition]

Rev. date: 10/07/2024

This book is dedicated to my wife who has made me re-realize my love of poetry, to my mother who has always said I could do better, to my father who encouraged my manliness, to my brother who made me realize I am an 80's kid who was born in the 90's, to my best friends who helped me enjoy life, and to my latest arrival – my son, Samuel Arthur – who has and will give me the most inspiration throughout my life.

JJBullfrog.com

Instagram: @jj_bullfrogstagram

Twitter/X: @BullfrogDusk

YouTube: JJ Bullfrog

Contents

Madame Morte 1
Sole 3
The Trash Man Cometh 5
Sunset 7
Found On A Stall Door In The Men's Bathroom 8
Total Travesty 9
Garbage Bag (Recycled) 11
Tangent 12
Free 15
Bob 17
Sudden Birth of Snow 19
Boss 21
Sacrifice and Leadership 23
Paid 25
Always Alive 27
Heart Query 29
Maybe 30
Round 1 - Boggle - Large Sue 31
Round 2 - Boggle - Legend of Weasley 33
Round 4 - Boggle - Ogrely Lonely 35
Broken Base 37
Asunder Down Under 39
Overgrowth 40
Only A Flesh Wound 41

Sold 43

They Say The King Is Dead. (Partially AI Generated) 44

Dew eye half two? 45

Suet 47

Linda H. 48

Random Thoughts of a Valvoline Customer 49

Secondhand Purchase 50

Pallets 51

From Seed to Plead 52

I Spit at You 53

untitled 54

Alcohol 55

Stretchy Banana 57

Nailed It 58

Two-minute Poem 59

Extraction 61

Worf is Missing. 62

Am I Late? 63

Caffeine 65

Like The Wheels of a Car 66

Remineralization 67

Lazy Hard Worker 68

Ode To Traffic 69

Squire 71

Torn Obligation 72

A Slice of Pilish 75

Greenhouse Chanty 76

Thanks Biden 77

Struggles of a Constipated Poet	79
Blue and Yellow	80
My Stomach Hurts	81
A Wonderful Day	83
Dark Honey	85
PDA	86
An Elegy	87
Stepping Up	89
Woodman	91
Motivation	93

Madame Morte

Wraithing hair and ice cold stare
Of wrathful women please beware.
Just for starts, they shrink your hearts
And break your soul in many shards.
One look and then your brighting grin
Will sour from their blighting chin.
To your demise her sunken eyes
Will show the truth of buried lies.
Relations said of pre-owned bed
Where many men have woke up dead.

Sole

Hmm...
What's a Soul?
A string for the heart!
A contact of shoe and ground,
Connection of Spirit and Body.

The Trash Man Cometh

Pounds of flesh ream.
The eyes are fastened,
Dreaming the dream,
The mind is relaxed,
Predicting a scheme.
Then, resonant thunder,
The cease of a scream.
The orbs are forced opened
By the great geared machine.
Bones creak with attack
To gravity's muse,
Trips over a table
And puts on his shoes.
Eminent rumbles
Grows louder each leap
As he crawls out the door
To meet the filth heap.

With a choke of demise,
The beast in view halts
By the red octagon
As it shutters its vaults.
He pulls the bin over
To the side of the road
And respectfully enters
His humble abode.
He takes off his shoes,
Stands up the board.
Lifts up the weight
On his bed off the floor.
The thunder desists,
The resounds are gone.
The brain hurries back
To vision of song
Of when the Trash Man Cometh.

Sunset

I would smile all the way down a cliff.
And I'd love the pain at the bottom.
And as I bleed, the sweet relief of my heart would be heavenly.
Don't ever set, sun.
Keep me alive in that moment at the bottom of the cliff.
Let me fall asleep, body broken.
Don't take me, sundown.

Found On A Stall Door In The Men's Bathroom

    Eat
      THe
         Soup.
    BuRn
      THe
         CaN.

                --OPEN
                  M!C

Total Travesty

There once was a girly
Who thought she was hip.
She hated her parents
And gave them her lip.
She went out the door
To walk to her school.
She thought she was hip
(She thought she was cool).
And as she stomped forth,
As she spat and she cuss,
Walked into the street
And got hit by a bus.

Garbage Bag (Recycled)

There once was a man named Jeremiah
Whose favorite fruit was juicy papaya.
But not to be at the very least rude,
The man loved to eat every kind of food.
He eats carrots and tomatoes,
Starchy buttered baked potatoes,
Pancakes with the syrup moisters,
Lumpy rocky mountain oysters,
Baking powder neutralizers,
Spicy chicken appetizers,
Salty fish and shrimp with Icees,
Grilled up cheeseburgers, and gou' cheese.
He's the rogue of picky eaters,
He eats hotdogs off the bleachers,
Eats ice cream off the rocky road,
Eats pizza pringles ala mode,
Wanted moon cheese, built a rocket,
Loves strawberries dipped in chocolate,
He believes brussel sprouts are cool,
Just thinking 'bout them makes him drool,
Fried rice and corn and straw and wheat,
Can even eat it off his feet,
Every berry (blue or boisen),
Doesn't care his food is poison,
So he died.

Tangent

Smite me.
A roller coaster ride with a bolt loose.
A bull's hoof suddenly caught on a train rail.
Driving a truck with a flat tire.
A bullet fired close to the ear.
The close call.
What is it I must do
To get to you,
An idiot?
A fool.
I fell asleep.
It wouldn't be such a deal
If my slumber wasn't at
The wheel.
You are alive,
Bruised?
Only in a couple places.
What did it cost me?
Only my transportation.
Only my occupation.
Only my pride.

What do you call these mishaps,
Kid?
A curve in my line.
A veering.
A tangent.
There must be a way to get back on track.
The door of opportunity doesn't knock itself.
You must buy the pass of readiness.
This is not the end.

Free

I took a bath.
No rhyme to support it,
Just a reason behind it:
I was feeling....
Hold up. What is a feeling? Maybe 'feeling' is
the wrong word to describe this....
I WAS dirty
And I was tired
On a day holy to select few that could include me.
The wife,
Blessed be her beautiful soul,
Told me I should take a bath.
But where should I take it?
There are no clubs in town.
Hmmmmmmm...

Anyway, I took my
Satisfying,
Sweaty,
Sultry dip, scrubbing my bod and bunions,
And pits that smelled like onions,
(Notice the tense of that word.
It's because I smell not of onions anymore, but I smell as a god...
Who uses a tea tree shampoo.)
Listening to VORW.
BUT
I am free. Free to free-ball it from the bath
to the bedroom without the
Disgust in a man's face and the
Scoffing of a woman.
Yes, this is frreeeddddooooommmmmm.

Bob

There once was a man named Bob
Who knew another man named Bob
Who knew another man named Bob
Who knew another man named Bob
Who was my Gramps.
They sat among lamps
Argue 'bout pre and post the most.
How fun
All the Bobs owned a gun
And shot targets in the desert just for
Kicks.
They had to use Vicks
On their lips, the desert makes lips dry,
But later on their hips,
'Cause you know they got old.
They call it Tiger Balm,
Or so I've been toooooold.
There... once was a man named Bob
Who knew another man named Bob
Who knew another man named Bob
Who knew another man named Bob
Who knew another man named Bawb
Who knew another man named Rawb
And they all knew a slawb
Who ate nothing more than corn on the
caawwwwwwww-AAAAAAAAWB!

Sudden Birth of Snow

Just a minute ago,
There was no snow.
And now the feathers of angels' pillows
Drift in a wet sleet creating billows
Of white, cleansing the colors of Earth,
Reminding me of hospital birth,
Which is not at all clean in the very least
Which is why gloves are used to protect kids from yeast.
(With that, I could find no more words to splay across this canvas about this very true event in the middle of March.)

Boss

He
Kills a room with the stare.
Mocks
Existence with that glare.
My
Spirit steps down the stair.
Life
Is found not to be fair.
Gary, where hath thy crown gone?
Thy baldness ever shineth in the dust-ridden light.
Dost thou polish thy head?
Hast thou rendered it so with a shave?
What
Does he mean with that eye?!
Is
My blunder that he spy?
His
Brows are furrowed like dark rye...

Problem

Is, I cannot lie.

Holy gates! Thy lips, stiffer than last night's drink they be.

Dost thou hast lockjaw?

Thou can eat? Will thou starve?

Let me grab mine viola, and strum a solemn tune for thee.

I

Can't stand this shadow.

Need

He stare at me so low?

To

The grave I shall go.

Pee

Now trickles on my toe.

Sacrifice and Leadership

Strength in their arms
Sitting parallel to each other
On their barstools.
Sipping fierce drinks
Not knowing who their neighbor is.
One bald with toned skin and bones,
One with wavy peppered hair and a team on his shirt,
Both stern, or stern looking,
Watching the game.
I know them well enough.
Their minds set on closure,
Both knowing it's far away.
Striving ceaselessly, set on a future goal.
You'll see it, but never find it.
Is it addiction? Is it passion?
You climb up the latter,
Slipping a little but never falling..

Until you do.

All do eventually.

You prize your workers.

You want them to have good lives

But you can only do so much.

What is your duty, then?

To keep them busy?

To keep climbing?

Have you plateaued?

Will we?

Is that why you're sipping fierce drinks?

Paid

Paid to talk
Paid to play
Paid to water
Paid to day.
Podcasts are interesting.
That's all they are.
Entertainment to work,
Listen to it in the car.
Vidya is great,
To stream it is hard.
Well, to find time to is.
But fun is the reward.
Growing is hot,
At least not without hats.
Short sleeves are cooler
But the sunburn's the shats.

Always Alive

Loving, selfish, curious creature,
Created out of wistful thinking,
Painless one with innocent tenure,
High honor guest with lowest ranking.
Prudence take you, bolding life.
Pain will find you, it's what you make of it.
Milk to steak and strength from strife,
The worst will come but you may love it.
The brightest sun, dim close to yours,
The greatest praise would make you laugh.
Someday a loving curious creature
Will bring you joy, the best to have.

Heart Query

To those who are like mountains:
What makes your heart steadfast?
How do you love and does it last?
Where is your bed and your bedrock lay?
How do you love and does it stay?
To those who are like fog:
Why do you drift and what is your goal?
How do you let the good times roll?
What is your aim for the work you put in?
Does the height of the mountains drive you to sin?
To those who are like the foundation:
Under the weight, do you only sink lower?
Do you care that you're used to found every tower?
Does your core crumble and weaken your will?
Is your back in pain from the shifts and the mill?
To those who are like springs:
Are you found under the mountain?
Are you free as a bird, have you sprung like a fountain?
Will you push your way through until you reach the valley?
Will you become like the river and flow to the ocean in a rally?

Maybe

Is there something wrong with being a
Wandering
M**o**nster;
Go**r**ging,
Mil**k**ing
Colla**p**sible
Flowc**h**arts,
Cancer**o**usly
Communa**l**ising
Aggravat**i**ons
Apoplecti**c**ally?

Round 1 - Boggle - Large Sue

Here's a small **Tot**
With a large thought:
'Did you know **This**?
I got to **Tow** sis.
Sue's the largest,
Like a **Nexus**.'
With grunts and **Huts**,
With **Nets** and gut,
They **Tase** the girl
To keep her mouth **Shut**.

Round 2 - Boggle - Legend of Weasley

My Weasley got too Hot.
Summer roads we drove.
The poor thing had a rot.
From his behind, he did Tove.
An appointment overdue
For the sickly Toot be met.
No Hoot given for, Too.
That's why we take him to the Vet.

Round 3 - Boggle - Asian Sports Discipline

Try my patience.
Rit the blackboard.
Sit on an uncomfortable stool
And show **Net** score.
Beat me with a **Riet**
To really **Turn** me on.
In **Tens** pain is my fate
Since all my **Yen** is gone.

Round 4 - Boggle - Ogrely Lonely

There's lives an ogre on the shore of a **Voe**
Whose **Snot** covered **Stony** face made all men row
Away from the inlet, surprise to the guy,
Since only the ogre knew one word... it's '**Bye**'.

Round 5 - Boggle - English Saying to Scottish Drunks

Don't **Tilt** your **Kilt**
For a **Tot**, you lot!

Broken Base

Like a statue
Figuratively tipped over
By the weight of the last day
And then pinned by a cold breeze
And the safety of a warm sheet,
I cannot get up.
The chill on my face,
A warning of icy doom
As soon as my feet
Meet the fuzzy floor,
Keeps me in this insufferable
Position.
May the chill of the morn
Be cursed.

Asunder Down Under

As a guy,
Look into mine eye,
And see that I
Do not like sticky thigh.
This sweat I drench
Comes with no wrench.
So this I beg,
No sticking leg,
Just boxer brief
Or olive leaf.
I swear I'll cry
If these legs ain't dry.

Overgrowth

I once considered you an undesirable ornament.
When I had to get rid of you, it made me lament,
Not because I loved you - I hated you with all my muster.
But with a bit of education, I now see every luster.
You can feed me and cure me, and make my yard look lovely.
And here I was just pulling you out because you were ugly.

Only A Flesh Wound

She found him in the lily pots
With a wound on his webbed toe.
She might be crazy silly-lots,
But her heart is made of gold.
She saved the gooey swamp friend
From the thing's untimely demise.
A friend of phibians' a friend of mine.
I consider a frog helper 'the wise'.
Even as a frog does nothing important,
You must know that they also hurt nothing.
Rare folk may consider them ugly,
Although, their true beauty's worth something.
Back to the story from the first pairs of lines
She surprised me with saving a second.
To keep a frog from being stepped on is kind
And their redeemer is to be reckoned…
With

Sold

The colored things behind cold steel...
Do you know and can you feel?
I often wonder about the meal
I give to you.
We breed you, then ween you slow.
You catch the sun enough to grow.
I provide your food, you know.
I live for you.
I weep to see you growing old.
I wish to only cut the mold
But I must do what I am told:
You cannot stay.
Violets blue and roses red,
I treat you well, you are well fed.
The wheels turn when there is dead
With every day.
Those of you who made the cut,
There is no grime. There is no mutt.
You'll have new homes with the doors shut.
You made it safe and sound.
Be alive when you're in the ground.

They Say The King Is Dead.
(Partially AI Generated)

The last of his blood-thirsty horde has been killed.
And all that remains are a few thousand men.
We band together with one thing fulfilled:
Under one banner to survive this world.
They murdered innocence in vain attempt
Of sacrifice to a destructive god.
Even their own blood they payed to preempt.
Irony disturbed thier lives, now exempt.
Unlike luck, we had planned from the start.
We worked to the bone to defeat the unrivaled.
We knew our decisions with map and chart.
For our innocent we tore them apart.
Although, we do not deserve the quiet.
The murderers condemn us to our realm.
Who are we to judge and deny it?
We need blood and the rest will supply it.
I cannot rest till I see his head
On a pike with his crown melted down.
How foolish that they say the king is dead
When survivors still turn our land red.
Our lives depend upon our will.
We shall not rest until all of them die.
The guts will be chopped, and bone to the mill.
Our vengeance be sweet for the blameless they kill.
May we finally find rest in our battle cry.

Dew eye half two?

   Won have, eye.
   Sidhe's ey have, to.
   Aye merry hur
   Bee caws sidhe kneads mi.
   Al sew, eye kneed hur.
   Wee nead won Ann ow there.
   Sew, eye dew.

Suet

Wife! What have you done...
The caged seed was for the birds
And here you eat it.

Linda H.

Knows how to catch amazing moments.

Random Thoughts of a Valvoline Customer

An oil change...
A change of the grease..
One contained mess for another.
It's somewhat like the change of the guard...
The guard change..
One professional slick - one slick professional..
For another.
Les grease monkey!
Why dost thou grease?
This luber has bumps on her torso...
Hmmmmmmmmmm..
A female greaser.
What has this world come to
That a female wants to do a monkey's job?
A monkey female? A femonkey?
Hmmmmmmmm..

Secondhand Purchase

Tumbling wet clothes dry.
I remember a day when
That was hard to do.

Pallets

The day continues
With these nightmares, thoughts haunted.
They're only vinca.

From Seed to Plead

I might as well explain
A theme I have presented.
I thought the plot was plain
But my riddles have a dent.
I think from thought to thought,
The bouncing brain beneath the hare,
My bright sole I have wrot
But meaning seeming isn't there.
In a humid house of green,
A greenhouse you will find I mean,
The flowers there are rich once seen,
From Marigolds to Jasmarine.
And I enjoy the work I do,
Growing treasures of the Earth.
A fine pleasure of the few
to see the blooming life from 'birth'.
Though my only thoughts are love
There is one thing that brings me pain.
My mind is fell from push to shove,
My face is muddled with salty rain
When they say I have to throw the plants away.
And that should be enough.
I love my job and they love me.
Sometimes I count it rough
Since I've seen those plants from seed.

I Spit at You

      I don't know the way,
      I must find their weeboo queen.
      Spiny anteaters...

untitled

To destroy life
Is to destroy yourself.

Alcohol

I don't need to get drunk.
You're my inebriation.
It's probably been said before
By some other love sick impersonation
But really I don't care to care.
This is the end-all way I feel.
The twinkle in your eye tells me
That what I say to you means a great deal
To you. I can rest knowing that
You love me and the balance is there:
In other words I'm sure you understand
I love you just the same, and that's fair.
Now I apologize how ever-clear this is.
Sometimes it's better than muddy water.
I'm filled to the brim of a Pimm's cup
And I'm not going to rhyme this last verse.

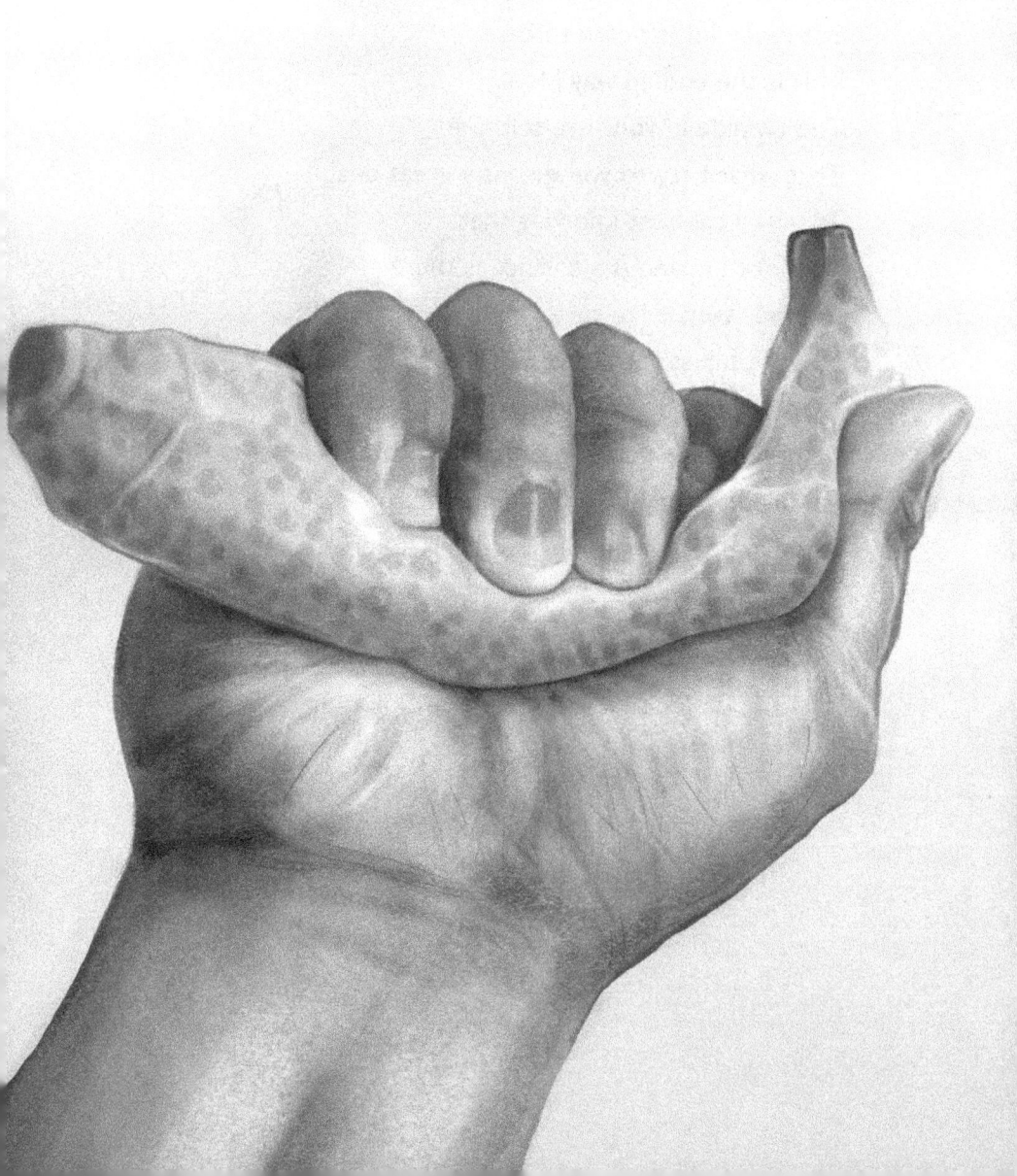

Stretchy Banana

I got it from a hobby store,
It's made of beads and rubber.
I don't know what I need it for,
I might be a sick bugger.
I squeeze it till it's pinky-size,
Why must banana suffer?

Nailed It

Ace... the Helpful Place.
These are the Hardwares of the Storeship Entreprise.
It's 5 hour mission:
To explore storage, new tools,
To seek out hardy tech
And new paint for my patio.
To boldly do what I need to do.
(Of course, there's only the case of the Primer Directive I have to worry about.)

Two-minute Poem

I'm about to go back to work.
I enjoyed my lunch, I swear.
Here's to the 30 minutes I got to sit down.
Working now is only fair.

Extraction

Wisdom lost, wisdom gained,
Bone baptized then ordained.
Templar made this holy site,
Pain now is my only blight.

Worf is Missing.

I am watching the low-budget younger brother
Of The Next Generation, Deep Space Nine...
As far as I'm concerned, seems to be less sex than TNG,
And trust me, for me, that's just fine.
I'm into the last episode of the first season
For a good reason, take my word.
I'm on a mission to watch all the Trekky stuff I can
Only getting up to make a turd.
We have an African-decended earth-born leader
On a station of majorly dull space men.
Together with his 'old man' parasitic friend
They command a space station, and then
We have a wrinkle-nosed major from Bajor
Who's in cahoots with a shape-shifting cop
Who is always picking on a thieving casino owner
Buttface, but here I should make a stop.
Seriously, I almost lost my breath there.
We have the station engineer, a fat man with curly hair,
Who's first purpose is his wife and kid.
His wife is the station teacher who only misses the feature
Of having a big mouth with a lid.
I came here for for Worf...
Where's Worf?

Am I Late?

Nah, fam.
I am an hour early.
Hot damn!
My toes are getting curly.
I found a hat next to the road
But it wasn't in the dirt.
Someone placed it on the fence
So that my head wouldn't be burnt.
Yes, they placed it there just for me.
Don't tell me that's highly unlikely!
It's on my head, right?
No, you..

Caffeine

I love to drink black coffee.
Nothing freshens better.
Everything gets fuzzy warm,
Exquisite to the letter.
Does coffee always taste good?
Today I made it right.
Obviously I love coffee,
To make it is delight.
As beautiful as this day,
Knowing who had made it,
Every bean that has been ground
Also been made to taste it.
Something feels askew.
Hello, I feel some tension.
I need to use the porcelain throne,
The need I should not mention.

Like The Wheels of a Car

I'm tired.

Like the back of the car
I'm exhausted.

Remineralization

Dentist, dentist, give me a break.
I pay your price so I don't end up in a lake.
The bottom is cold, and so is my money.
I'd rather use it to buy a house for me and my honey.
Dentist, dentist, you made holes in my pants.
You fill the holes in my head but now I can't dance.
Even an x-ray is exorbitant extreme.
The more you fist my pocket, the more I ream.
Dentist, dentist, is there another way
To get rid of disease and tooth decay?
If there is, can you tell me, please?
One patient won't kill your rich life of ease...

Lazy Hard Worker

I call myself Workaholic, but
A change of thought, like a frog
Gradually boiled in a pot of water,
Has changed me and I wish to revert
Back to the passions of hard work
That gives me thirst for life,
An unquenchable desire
For every good experience
Of loss and gain.
I am in essence a lazy hard worker.

Ode To Traffic

Forgo all thoughts of peace
Usurpers of my lane!
Certainly, thou whilst understand
Kindness when I bestow thee pain.
Yearnings of violence I have had for so long,
Over the brights and the blights born out of dumbness,
Under the care of detestable parents.

Squire

We stopped at the edge of an ocean of trees.
I wanted to follow you into the darkness.
'Go home, squire. My house needs your caring.'
The Woods of Fear you entered so daring.
Theo, Sir Theo, alive you may be.
I knew in my mind I was only a novice.
I asked to trudge with you, you didn't agree.
You'll never know what my heart was bearing.
I wanted to follow you into the darkness.
Theo, Sir Theo, alive you may be.
I came to the castle, two men found unconscious.
Wooster and Worcest I woke with my blaring:
'Help the knight, Theo! This is my grim plea.
The Woods of Fear he entered so daring.
Theo, Sir Theo, alive he may be.'
The refuge of death, the grave and disease,
We met at the edge a being most monstrous,
Hairless and pallid, the men it was scaring.
I wanted to follow you into the darkness.

Theo, Sir Theo, alive you may be.
It swore that my knight fought with all of his sharpness,
Defeated and beaten, the Skeleton King,
Stole a horse of the beast it was swearing.
The Woods of Fear you entered so daring.
Theo, Sir Theo, alive you may be.
The next day, my knight, I did as I promised.
I started to work when I found something staring.
The creature had followed me back whenst I flee.
I wanted to follow you into the darkness.
The Woods of Fear you entered so daring.
Theo, Sir Theo, alive you may be.

Torn Obligation

She makes it a refuge, the bed where I lay,
Beauty and sanctioned by God with a ring.
They need me at work but she wants me to stay.
Toil and stresses abound in the day.
At home she is there to rebalm the dread sting.
She makes it a refuge, the bed where I lay.
Invested in work, I start this Monday,
I've rested my weekend and feel like a king.
They need me at work but she wants me to stay.
Her hair is as soft as a lofty parfait.
Her heart is my hearth and to her I will cling.
She makes it a refuge, the bed where I lay.
A deluge of duty, they swear to dismay,
My refuge is work they spit and they sing.
They need me at work but she wants me to stay.
Her touch is what makes my soul silently play
Her kiss is the free flutter of the dove's wing
She makes it a refuge, the bed where I lay.
They need me at work but she wants me to stay.

A Slice of Pilish

"ASS I quip,"
I
Write complexly
To
Puzzle yours and minds.
Apparent slapstick wording structure...
See me,
The struggle from simple
Is ending here now.
The function
Can be elating.
Suffering comes *0 to everyone.

Greenhouse Chanty

This is not a taxi dude
Get off my wand
Get off my wand
This is not a taxi dude
You stupid fungus gnat

Thanks Biden

    Waiting in line
    With nonexistent blunt in my hand
    Hanging outside my window
    Outside the Valvoline.
    Why are they so slow?

Struggles of a Constipated Poet

Mall with a restroom
For rhyme and a load.
Solemn as a tomb,
What a time for an ode.

Blue and Yellow

Conformity surrounds me.

My Stomach Hurts

Grape juice in the morning and nothing to eat,
A stomach envenomed by lazy extention.
I did serve the family the eggs I did beat,
To not do it for me was not my intention.
I sat on the couch and mined in a dungeon,
Pay no attention to the rumbling craw
Until the food pouch rumbles in ruckerous gumbshin
And I sit up from pain by it's hungering claw.
Too late to scrounge, I gather my jacket,
Putting my boots on one foot at a skurk.
I rush to the truck, groaning a racket,
And I carpool with Bonnie, to her and my work.
From this short story, a short moral begs:
Stay away from the grape juice and scramble your eggs.

A Wonderful Day

The foggy morning drive was bliss,
My passenger was who I Missed.
The venture wasn't anything new
- Except for the future dew.
As we rode for monetary,
She mentioned something I had said
About a morning just like this,
"Perfect day for the walking dead..."
It's a wonderful day for a zombie apocalypse!
Remember to bring your holsters for your hips
As we sit on the porch and watch and lock our lips.
It's a wonderful day for a zombie apocalypse!

Dark Honey

Honey takes time to make
When a flower is nowhere seen.
In my case, I just got lazy,
Sleeping in my 'sectopod'.
But here it is, come taste its sweetness.
I found the nectar from a carcass.
Don't judge me...
I wanted to try something new.

PDA

White dress, flowing hair.
My wife, this is why I stare.
I love only you.

An Elegy

Here's to the death of a single man in the strong arms of the Klondike,
And two souls stood defiant in his place with a thirst to serve family.
Armed with abounding potential, but smote by a woman of beauty;
Accept sweet death's caress, your grave has collapsed for room for the womb.

Stepping Up

I need to earn money
And that comes with change:
A drop of psychotic,
A smidge of derange;
Derailment of sanity,
A kick in the butt,
A charring of function,
Hot blood from a cut;
Charcuterie bed,
B12 in the stream,
Sulpher and sweat,
Fleshy fresh steam;
An axe to the grindstone,
Screws to the chalk,
And mostly earn money
From walking the talk!

Woodman

I won the awesome love of a woman,
No one, especially me, saw it comin',
It's brought me to be a saw-surfin' woodman,
And after two years she has me in her womb,
I signed her up to get green from my tomb,
So if my fate's sealed, it won't be her doom.
And speaking of, traffick's a doom.
These death-dealing drivers are after my woman!
I can't be going off into that tomb
Just yet since a miracle's comin'.
My kin is neatly tucked in her womb,
And the babe must see me as a woodman.
However, can I call myself 'Woodman'?
Is this poorman's wage my family's doom?
We planned, nay, God planned this kid in the womb!
God planned the time I would love this woman!
The guy in the sky saw it comin'...
He plans life and he plans the depth of my tomb.
There's no strategy for the time of the tomb.
You can try to invest with the wage of a woodman.

But who in the world sees it comin'?
Only a fool says he's preparing for doom.
Only a fool can say he's got eye for a woman.
Only a fool leaves after he takes up her womb.
It's hard to make room for the womb.
The space in the house we call an office is a tomb.
I must organize it for the baby and woman.
I have plenty of time as a woodcutting woodman.
Every time I enter, there's only doom.
The minimalist in me did not see it comin'.
A life of conformation I couldn't see comin',
I'm as dumb as my time to come out of the womb.
I won't let this freedom bring me to doom,
For the likes of my wife, I must reach out from my tomb.
I must go the distance as a blade-dancing woodman,
A two-timing hard working man for my woman!
Mandatory doom, know that it's comin'.
Love the love of your woman, with that child in her womb.
I'll be here 'til the tomb, as of now...
I'm you're woodman.

Motivation

The piper is lost
And the stork has been called.
The pan hears the bells,
The fairy has fallen.
The priest is excited
Yet not as much nervous
To see the new life
He helped bring to service.

Hello, thanks for reading my book. I know it was a lot to handle. Make sure to color in the illustrations. Send them to me on any of the social media pages on the preface. Yeah, I know. The pictures are not the best. Haha! I think they add a bit of heartfelt umami to my poetry. Anyway, did you see the neck they drew for me for "Garbage Bag (Recycled)"? Kill it with fire! No, really, I appreciate everyone who masticated my work. If it was like gum or a sultry sirloin, I hope you enjoyed it. Make sure to go through them again. I added secret word play for some of my poems. Let me know what you think.

Thanks again,
Jeremiah "Bullfrog" Wilmot

www.ingramcontent.com/pod-product-compliance
Lightning Source LLC
Chambersburg PA
CBHW031652040426
42453CB00006B/281